## ACKNOWLEDGEMENTS

A big thanks to all my team who have made such a huge effort to make this such a beautiful book and without whose support it would not have been possible.

**Rhiannon, Dionne & Nicole at Designer Yarns:** for doing such a good job in getting the yarn to me and organising the book production.

**Janice Issitt:** our wonderful photographer, for her inspiring images and great eye for a good shot.

**Camilla Perkins:** my gorgeous daughter and talented stylist; for great planning and attention to detail and style.

**Besh & Chris Grimes:** for the wonderful location and letting us photograph in and around their beautiful Sussex farmhouse and to Jane Eakhurst from Serendipity Reclamation.

**Beryl Oakes:** my mum and crochet connoisseur.

**Emily Brown:** our stunning model.

**Pat Clough:** our fantastic layout designer for putting together the images and text to make this a beautiful book.

**Ian Watt at Designer Yarns:** for having faith in my ability in doing justice to Noro Yarns.

# CONTENTS

DESIGN SEVEN | PAGE 26 | BOBBLE HAT

DESIGN TEN | PAGE 29 | SHELL & LACE HEADBAND

DESIGN THIRTEEN | PAGE 34 | SUMMER GARDEN THROW

DESIGN EIGHT | PAGE 27 | BERRY CUSHION COVER

DESIGN TWELVE | PAGE 32 | HYDRANGEA TABLECLOTH

DESIGN NINE | PAGE 28 | BOBBLE SCARF

DESIGN ELEVEN | PAGE 30 | DEVINE DEVICE COVER

DESIGN ONE

## LACE SHAWL

DESIGN TWO
FINGERLESS GLOVES

DESIGN THREE

# BEADED PETAL CUSHION COVER

DESIGN FOUR

# PRESERVE DELIGHTS

DESIGN FIVE

# TABLE RUNNER

DESIGN SIX

# POM POM BUGGY BLANKET

DESIGN SEVEN
BOBBLE HAT

DESIGN EIGHT

# BERRY CUSHION COVER

DESIGN NINE

# BOBBLE SCARF

DESIGN TEN

# SHELL & LACE HEADBAND

DESIGN ELEVEN

# DEVINE DEVICE COVER

DESIGN TWELVE

# HYDRANGEA TABLECLOTH

DESIGN THIRTEEN
SUMMER GARDEN THROW

DESIGN ONE

# LACE SHAWL

### Materials

4 x 50g balls Noro Taiyo 4ply, shade S30
Size 4.5mm crochet hook

### Size

**Finished measurement:**
approx 37cm x 188cm (14½in x 74in)

### Tension

18 sts and 9 rows to 10cm (4in) square working trebles using 4.5mm crochet hook.
It is essential to work to the correct tension. If there are less stitches, use a thinner hook, if there are more stitches, use a thicker hook.

### Abbreviations

**ch** chain
**ch sp** chain space
**dc** double crochet
**rep** repeat
**RS** right side
**ss** slip stitch
**st(s)** stitch(es)
**sp** space
**tr** treble
**WS** wrong side
**2trCL** (Two treble cluster) yrh, insert hook in sp, yrh, pull yarn through, yrh, pull yarn through 2 loops, yrh, insert hook in same sp, yrh, pull yarn through, yrh, pull yarn through 2 loops (3 loops on hook), yrh, pull yarn through all 3 loops on hook.

## SHAWL

Make 85ch.

**Row 1:** (RS) 7tr in 10th ch from hook (shell), *1ch, miss 4ch, [1tr, 1ch] in next ch, miss 4ch, 7tr in next ch; rep from * ending [1ch, 1tr] in last ch.

**Row 2:** 4ch, 1tr in first tr, *1ch, miss next 2tr (of shell), 1tr in each of next 3tr, 1ch, miss next ch sp, [1tr, 3ch, 1tr (V)] in top of next 1tr; rep from * ending [1tr, 1ch, 1tr] in last ch sp.

**Row 3:** 3ch, 3tr in first ch sp, *1ch, miss next ch sp, [1tr, 1ch] in second tr of next 3tr group (centre st), miss next 1ch sp, 7tr in next 3ch sp (in centre of V); rep from * ending 4tr in last ch sp.

**Row 4:** 3ch, miss first tr, 1tr in next tr, 1ch, miss next 2tr and next ch sp, [1tr, 3ch, 1tr] in next tr, *1ch, miss next ch sp and next 2tr, 1tr in each of next 3 tr, 1ch, miss next 2tr and next ch sp, [1tr, 3ch, 1tr] in next tr; rep from * ending miss next 2tr (1st 2tr of last shell), 1tr in last tr, 1tr in top of first 3ch.

**Row 5:** 4ch, miss first ch sp, *7tr in next ch sp (centre of V), 1ch, miss next ch sp, [1tr, 1ch] in second tr of next 3tr group (centre st), miss next ch sp; rep from * ending 7tr in centre of last V, 1ch, 1tr in top of first 3ch.

Rep Rows 2-5 until shawl measures 175cm (69in) ending on a Row 5. Do not fasten off.

## EDGING

**Row 1:** (WS) 4ch, 1tr in first tr, miss next ch sp, miss next 3tr, *[2trCL, 3ch, 2trCL] in next tr (middle of shell), miss next 3tr, miss next ch sp, [1tr, 3ch, 1tr] in next tr, miss next ch sp, miss next 3tr; rep from * to last ch sp, [1tr, 1ch, 1tr] in last ch sp.

**Row 2:** (RS) 4ch, 1tr in first ch sp, *[2trCL, 3ch, 2trCL] in next 3ch sp, [1tr, 3ch, 1tr] in next 3ch sp; rep from * ending [1tr, 1ch, 1tr] in last ch sp.

**Row 3:** 1ch, 1dc in first tr, 2ch, *[5tr, 2ch] in next 3ch sp (between clusters), [1dc, 2ch] in next 3 ch sp (between trebles); rep from * ending 1dc in last ch sp.

**Row 4:** 1ss in first dc, *1ch, [1dc in next tr, 3ch, ss in first of 3ch,] 4 times, 1dc in next tr, 3ch, ss in first of 3ch, ss in same dc, 1ch, ss in next dc; rep from * ending 1dc in last st.

Fasten off.

Working on underside of first 85ch at other end of shawl with RS facing, join yarn in first ch sp.

**Row 1:** (RS) 3ch, 1tr in same sp. *[2trCL, 3ch, 2trCL] in bottom sp of 7tr shell, [1tr, 3ch, 1tr] in bottom of next 1tr; rep from * to last sp, [1tr, 1ch, 1tr] in 4th of first 10 ch from Row 1.

**Row 2:** (WS) 4ch, 1tr in first ch sp, [2trCL, 3ch, 2trCL] in next 3ch sp, [1tr, 3ch, 1tr] in next 3ch sp; rep from * ending [1tr, 1ch, 1tr] in last ch sp.

**Row 3:** 1ch, 1dc in first tr, 2ch, *[5tr, 2ch] in next 3ch sp (between clusters), [1dc, 2ch] in next 3 ch sp (between trebles); rep from * ending 1dc in last ch sp.

**Row 4:** 1ss in first dc, *1ch, [1dc, in next tr, 3ch, ss in first of 3ch,] 4 times, 1dc in next tr, 3ch, ss in first of 3ch, ss in same dc, 1ch, ss in next dc; rep from * ending 1dc in last st.

Fasten off.

## FINISHING

Sew in ends.

DESIGN TWO

# FINGERLESS GLOVES

### Materials

2 x 50g balls of Noro Silk Garden, shade 389
Size 4mm and 5mm crochet hooks
6 x Size 6 seed beads, pale pink

### Size

To fit an average-size woman's hand

### Tension

15 sts and 12 rows to 10cm (4in) square working htr using 4mm crochet hook.
It is essential to work to the correct tension. If there are less stitches, use a thinner hook, if there are more stitches, use a thicker hook.

### Abbreviations

| | |
|---|---|
| **approx** | approximately |
| **ch** | chain |
| **cont** | continu(e)(ing) |
| **dc** | double crochet |
| **htr** | half treble |
| **rep** | repeat |
| **RS** | right side |
| **ss** | slip stitch |
| **st(s)** | stitch(es) |
| **tr** | treble |
| **yrh** | yarn round hook |
| **dc2tog** | (double crochet two stitches together) [insert hook in next st, yrh, pull yarn through] twice, yrh, pull through all 3 loops on hook (one stitch decreased) |
| **htr2tog** | (half treble 2 stitches together) [yrh, insert hook in next st, yrh, pull yarn through] twice, yrh, pull through all 5 loops on hook (one stitch decreased). |

### Pattern Note

This pattern is worked in the round, place a stitch marker in the beginning loop of each round, starting at Round 1.
There are also two different stitch markers for the thumb position on increasing rounds, use a contrasting colour for these markers.

## GLOVE

Starting at wrist end.

Using 5mm hook, make 32ch, join with a ss in first ch to form a ring. Place st marker (count marked st as last st)

## WRIST

**Round 1:** (RS) 1dc in each ch to end. (32 sts)

Change to size 4mm hook. Cont in rounds with RS always facing.

**Round 2:** Htr2tog, 1htr in each of next 14 sts, htr2tog, 1htr in each st to end. (30 sts)

Continue to work in a spiral rounds:

**Round 3:** (Pattern) *Miss 2 sts, 2htr in each of next 2 sts; rep from * until work measures 8.5cm (3¼in) - approx 6 rows of pattern.

## HAND

**Round 1:** 1htr in each of next 12 sts, 2htr in next st (place thumb marker in first of these 2htr), 1htr in next st, 2htr in next st (place second thumb marker in last of these 2htr), 1htr in each st to end. (32 sts)

**Round 2:** 1htr in each st to end. (32 sts)

**Round 3:** 1htr in each st to first thumb marker, 2htr in next st – the one with thumb marker – (place thumb marker in first of these 2htr), 1htr in each st to next thumb marker, 2htr in next st – the one with thumb marker – (place second thumb marker in last of these 2htr), 1htr in each st to end of round. (34 sts)

**Round 4:** 1htr in each st to first thumb marker, 2htr in next st (place thumb marker in first of these 2tr), 1htr in each st to next thumb marker, 2htr in next st (place second thumb marker in last of these 2htr), 1htr in each st to end. (36 sts)

**Round 5:** 1htr in each st to end. (36 sts)

**Round 6:** 1htr in each st to first thumb marker, 2htr in next st (place thumb marker in first of these 2htr), 1htr in each st to next thumb marker, 2htr in next st (place second thumb marker in last of these 2htr), 1htr in each st to end. (38 sts)

**Round 7:** 1htr in each st to first thumb marker, 2htr in next st (place thumb marker in first of these 2htr), 1htr in each st to next thumb marker, 2htr in next st (place second thumb marker in last of these 2htr), 1htr in each st to end. (40 sts)

**Round 8:** 1htr in each st to first thumb marker, miss 13 sts, 1htr in next st, 1htr in each st to end. (27 sts)

Remove thumb stitch markers only.

Do not remove st marker to indicate beg of round.

**Round 9:** 1htr in each st to last 2 sts, htr2tog. (26 sts)

**Round 10:** 1htr in each st to end. (26 sts)

**Round 11:** 1dc in each st to end, join with a ss in last st.

Fasten off.

## THUMBHOLE

With RS facing and using 4mm hook, join yarn with a ss in first st of 13 sts missed for thumbhole in Round 8.

**Round 1:** (RS) 1ch, 1dc in same place. Place stitch marker. 1dc in each of next 12 sts around thumbhole. (13 sts)

Cont to work thumb in rounds with RS always facing.

**Rounds 2:** 1dc in first dc (with stitch marker), 1dc in each each st to last 2 sts, dc2tog. (12 sts)

**Round 3:** 1dc in each st to last st, 1ss in last st.

Fasten off.

## WRIST EDGING

With RS facing and using size 4mm hook, join yarn with a ss in underside of first chain at wrist end of glove.

**Round 1:** (RS) 1ch, make 30dc evenly around, join with a ss in first dc. (30 sts)

**Round 2:** (RS) 1ch, 1dc in same st, *3ch, ss in first of 3ch, miss 1 st, 1dc in next st; rep from * to end. Join with a ss in first 1dc.

Fasten off.

## BOW **(make two)**

Using size 4mm hook, make 16ch, join with a ss to form a ring.

**Round 1:** (RS) 1ch (does not count as a st), 1dc in each st to end, join with a ss in first dc. (16 sts).

**Round 2:** 3ch, (counts as tr), 1tr in each st to end; join with a ss in top of first 3ch. (16 sts).

**Round 3:** 1ch (does not count as a st), 1dc in each st to end, join with a ss in first dc.

Fasten off leaving a tail of approx 45cm (17½in)

## FINISHING

Thread 3 beads onto yarn tail.

Wrap yarn around centre of ring tightly to create bow shape, placing the 3 beads in a row on the last wrap and secure in place. Attach bow to front of Glove in centre, positioned at wrist.

DESIGN THREE

# BEADED PETAL CUSHION COVER

### Materials
5 x 50g balls of Noro Silk Garden, shade 338
Approx 20 size 6 seed beads (pearl)
41cm (16in) square cushion pad.
Size 4mm crochet hook

### Size
**Finished measurement:** 41cm x 41cm (16in x 16in)

### Tension
12 sts and 15 rows to 10cm (4in) square working double crochets using 4.5mm crochet hook.
It is essential to work to the correct tension. If there are less stitches, use a thinner hook, if there are more stitches, use a thicker hook.

### Abbreviations

| | |
|---|---|
| **dc** | double crochet |
| **rep** | repeat |
| **ss** | slip stitch |
| **tr** | treble |
| **ch** | chain |
| **st(s)** | stitch(es) |

## FRONT AND BACK **(both alike)**
Make 52 ch.
**Row 1:** 1dc in second ch from hook, 1dc in each st to end. (51 sts)
**Row 2:** 1ch, 1dc in each st to end.
Rep Row 2 until work measures 41cm (16in).
Fasten off.

## EDGING
**Round 1:** Pin front and back with wrong sides together. Join yarn in one st away from one of the corners. 1ch, make 51 dcs evenly along first side, joining both pieces together. *3dc in corner st, make 51 dcs evenly along next side; rep from * to end of third edge. 3dc in corner st, insert cushion pad, 51 dcs evenly along fourth side enclosing cushion pad, 3dc in corner st. Join with a ss in first dc.
Remove pins.
**Round 2: (picot edge)** 1ch, 1dc in same st, *3ch, ss in third ch from hook, miss 1 st, 1dc in next st; rep from * to end, ending 1ss in first dc.
Fasten off.

## FLOWERS **(make 3)**
Make 6 ch, join with a ss in first ch to form a ring.
**Round 1:** 1ch, 15dc in ring, join with a ss in first dc.
**Round 2:** 3ch, 1tr in same st, 1tr in next st, 3ch, 1ss in next st, *3ch, 1tr in each of next 2 tr, 3ch, 1ss in next st; rep from * 3 more times, working last ss in first dc.
(5 petals)
Fasten off.

## FINISHING
Sew three flowers to corner of one side of cushion.
Hand sew 6 or 7 beads into the centre of each flower.

DESIGN FOUR

# PRESERVE DELIGHTS

## Materials
1 x 50g ball of Noro Silk Garden, shade 366 (makes approx 3 covers)
3 x elasticated bands
3 x 50cm (20in) lengths of narrow ribbon
50 beads per cover, seed beads size 6, white
Size 4mm crochet hook

## Size
**Approx** 16cm (6¼in) diameter

## Tension
15 sts and 12 rows to 10cm (4in) square working htr using 4mm crochet hook.
It is essential to work to the correct tension. If there are less stitches, use a thinner hook, if there are more stitches, use a thicker hook.

## Abbreviations

| | | | |
|---|---|---|---|
| **approx** | approximately | **P2B** | place two beads |
| **ch** | chain | **rep** | repeat |
| **cont** | continu(e)(ing) | **RS** | right side |
| **dc** | double crochet | **ss** | slip stitch |
| **htr** | half treble | **st(s)** | stitch(es) |

## PRESERVE COVER
Using 4mm hook, make 6 ch, join with a ss in first ch to form a ring.
**Round 1: (RS)** 2ch (counts as first htr), 11htr in ring, join with a ss in top of first 2ch. (12 sts).
Cont in rounds with RS always facing.
**Round 2:** 2ch (counts as first htr), 1htr in same place as last ss, 2htr in each st to end, join with a ss in top of first 2ch. (24 sts)
**Round 3:** 2ch (counts as first htr), *2htr in each of next 2 sts, 1htr in next st; rep from * to end, join with a ss in top of first 2ch. (40 sts)
**Round 4:** 2ch (counts as first htr), 1htr in same place as last ss, *1htr in each of next 3 sts, 2htr in next st; rep from * to last 3 sts, 1htr in each of last 3 sts, join with a ss in top of first 2ch. (50 sts)
**Round 5:** 2ch (counts as first htr), 1htr in same place as last ss, *1htr in each of next 4 sts, 2htr in next st; rep from * to last 4 sts, 1htr into each of last 4 sts, join with a ss in top of first 2ch. (60 sts)
**Round 6:** 2ch (counts as first htr), 1htr in same place as last ss, *1htr in each of next 5 sts, 2htr in next st; rep from * to last 5 sts, 1htr in each of last 5 sts, join with a ss in top of first 2ch. (70 sts)
**Round 7:** 2ch (counts as first htr), 1htr in same place as last ss, *1htr in each of next 6 sts, 2htr in next st; rep from * to last 6 sts, 1htr in each of last 6 sts, join with a ss in top of first 2ch. (80 sts)
Fasten off.

## EDGING
Thread beads onto yarn (50 beads per cover).
Working on WS join yarn in any st, 1ch, 1dc in same st. *2ch, P2B, 1ch, ss in third ch from hook, miss 1 st, 1dc in each of next 2 sts; rep from * to end.
Fasten off.

## FINISHING
Place Preserve Cover over lid of jar, secure with elastic band and decorate with ribbon.

DESIGN FIVE

# TABLE RUNNER

### Materials

4 x 50g balls of Noro Taiyo 4ply shade S30
20 size 6 seed beads (pearl)
Size 4mm crochet hook

### Size

**Finished measurement:**
Approx 167.5cm x 30cm (66in x 12in)

### Tension

18 sts and 8 rows to 10cm (4in) square working trebles using 4mm crochet hook.
It is essential to work to the correct tension. If there are less stitches, use a thinner hook, if there are more stitches, use a thicker hook.

### Abbreviations

| | | | |
|---|---|---|---|
| **dc** | double crochet | **ss** | slip stitch |
| **ch** | chain | **sp** | space |
| **ch sp** | chain space | **st(s)** | stitch(es) |
| **PB** | Place bead | **tr** | treble |
| **dc2tog** | (double crochet two stitches together) [insert hook in next st, yrh, pull yarn through] twice, yrh, pull through all 3 loops on hook (one stitch decreased) | | |

## TABLE RUNNER

Make 57 ch.
Row 1: 1dc in second ch from hook, 1dc in each ch to end. (56 sts).
Row 2: 4ch, *miss 3 sts, 3tr in next st, 1ch; rep from * to last 4 sts, 1tr in last st.
Row 3: 3ch, 2tr in first ch sp, 1ch, *3tr in next ch sp, 1ch; rep from * to last ch sp, 1tr in top of 3ch from previous Row.
Row 4: 3ch, 2tr in first ch sp, 1ch, *3tr in next ch sp, 1ch; rep from * to last ch sp, 3tr, 1ch in last ch sp, 1tr in top of first 3ch from previous Row.
Rep Row 4 until work measures approx 160cm (63in) or length required for table.
Fasten off.

## EDGING

### SHORT EDGES (widths)

Thread 20 beads onto yarn.

#### First Short Edge

Row 1: (RS) Join yarn in first st, 1ch, 1dc in first ch sp, *1dc in each of next 3 sts, 1dc in next ch sp; rep from * ending 1dc in last 2 sts. (51 sts).
Row 2: 1ch, 1dc in first st, *5ch, ss in third ch from hook, 3ch, miss next 4 sts, 1dc in next dc; rep from * to end.
Row 3 (bead row): 1ch, 1dc in first st, *5ch, PB, 1ch, ss in third ch from hook, 4ch, 1dc in next st (dc); rep from * to end. Fasten off.

#### Second Short Edge

Row 1: (RS) Working on underside of chains from first Row, join yarn in first st, 1ch, 1dc in same st, *dc2tog, 1dc in each of next 9 sts; rep from * to end. (51 sts).
Repeat Rows 2-3 from First Edge.

## EDGING

### LONG EDGES (lengths)

#### First Long Edge

Row 1: (RS) Working along length of work, join yarn in side of first double crochet row of End Edging, 1ch, *2dc in next ch sp, 1dc in sp between side of tr and ch from tr group; rep from * end, ending 1dc in side of dc from End Edging Row.
Row 2: 1ch, 1dc in next and each st to end, ending 1dc in each row edge of End Edging.

#### Second Long Edge

Row 1: (RS) Working along second length of work, join yarn in side of first double crochet row of Short Edge, 1ch, 1dc in each of next 2 end rows of Short Edge; rep from * from Row 1 First Long Edge.
Rep Row 2 from First Long Edge.
Fasten off.

## FINISHING

Sew in ends.

DESIGN SIX

# POM POM BUGGY BLANKET

**Materials**
5 x 50g balls of Noro Kureyon, shade 284
Size 5mm crochet hook

**Size**
**Finished measurement:** 66cm x 51cm (26in x 20in)

**Abbreviations**

| | | | |
|---|---|---|---|
| **ch** | chain | **ss** | slip stitch |
| **dc** | double crochet | **st(s)** | stitch(es) |
| **patt(s)** | pattern(s) | **tr** | treble |
| **rep** | repeat | **WS** | wrong side |
| **RS** | right side | **yrh** | yarn round hook |
| **CL** | (cluster) *yrh, insert hook in next st, yrh, pull yarn through, yrh, pull through 2 loops, work from * to * over the number of sts given on patt rows, yrh and pull through all loops on hook. | | |

**Tension**
13 sts and 6 rows to 10cm (4in) square working trebles using 5mm crochet hook.
It is essential to work to the correct tension. If there are less stitches, use a thinner hook, if there are more stitches, use a thicker hook.

## BLANKET

Make 77 ch.
**Row 1:** 1dc in 2nd ch from hook, 1dc in next ch, *miss 3 ch, 7tr in next ch, miss 3 ch, 1dc in each of next 3 ch; rep from * to last 4 ch, miss 3 ch, 4tr in last ch.
**Row 2: (RS)** 1ch, 1dc in each of first 2 sts, *3ch, 1CL over next 7 sts, 3ch, 1dc in each of next 3 sts; rep from * to last 4 sts, 3ch, 1CL over last 4 sts.
**Row 3:** 3ch (counts as 1tr), 3tr in top of 4trCL, *miss 3 ch, 1dc in each of next 3 dc, miss 3 ch, 7tr in closing loop of next CL; rep from * to end, finishing miss 3 ch, 1dc in each of last 2 dc.
**Row 4:** 3ch (counts as 1tr) miss first st, 1CL over next 3 sts, *3ch, 1dc in each of next 3 sts, 3ch, 1CL over next 7 sts; rep from * to end, finishing 3ch, 1dc in next st, 1dc in 3-ch from previous row.
**Row 5:** 1ch, 1dc in each of first 2 dc, *miss 3 ch, 7tr in closing loop of next CL, miss 3 ch, 1dc in each of next 3 dc; rep from * to end, finishing miss 3 ch, 4tr in top of 3-ch from previous row.
Rep Rows 2 – 5 until work measures approx 64cm (25in) ending on a Row 2.
Do not fasten off.

## EDGING

**Round 1: (RS of Short Edge)** 1ch, *make 70 dc evenly to the next corner, 3dc in corner st, make 88 dc evenly along Long Edge to next corner, 3dc in corner st; rep from * to last corner, 3dc in corner, join with a ss in first 1ch.
**Round 2: (RS)** 1ch, *1dc in each st to corner, 3dc in corner st; rep from * to end, join with a ss in first 1ch.
Fasten off.

## FINISHING

Make 4 small pom poms and attach one to each corner.

DESIGN SEVEN

# BOBBLE HAT

### Materials
Noro Silk Garden, shade 337
2[3] x 50g balls
Size 6mm crochet hook

### Size
50[54.4]cm (20[21¾]in) circumference

### Abbreviations

| | |
|---|---|
| **approx** | approximately |
| **ch** | chain |
| **cont** | continu(e)(ing) |
| **htr** | half treble |
| **rep** | repeat |
| **RS** | right side |
| **ss** | slip stitch |
| **st(s)** | stitch(es) |

### Tension
11 sts and 9 rows to 10cm (4in) square working half trebles using 6mm crochet hook and two strands of yarn.
It is essential to work to the correct tension. If there are less stitches, use a thinner hook, if there are more stitches, use a thicker hook.

### Pattern Note
Hat is made starting from top down and worked in a spiral.
Mark the beginning and end of each round by inserting a stitch marker in loop on hook at the beginning of each round.

## HAT
Using a double strand of yarn throughout (two balls of yarn) and 6mm hook.

**Round 1: (RS)** 2ch (does not count as st), 10htr in 3rd ch from hook. (10 sts)

Cont in rounds with RS always facing.

**Round 2:** Miss first 2ch, 2htr in each st to end. (20 sts).

**Round 3:** *1htr in next st, 2htr in next st; rep from * to end. (30 sts).

**Round 4:** *1htr in each of next 5 sts, 2htr in next st; rep from * to end. (35 sts).

**Round 5:** *1htr in each of next 6 sts, 2htr in next st; rep from * to end. (40 sts).

**Round 6:** *1htr in each of next 7 sts, 2htr in next st; rep from * to end. (45 sts).

***Small size only:***

**Round 7:** *1htr in each of next 8 sts, 2htr in next st; rep from * to end. (50 sts).

**Round 8 - 15:** 1htr in each st to end.

***Large size only:***

**Next Round:** *1htr in each of next 4 sts, 2htr in next st; rep from * to end. (36 sts)

**Round 4(5):** *1htr in each of next 5 sts, 2htr in next st; rep from * to end. (35/42 sts)

**Round 5(6):** *1htr in each of next 6 sts, 2htr in next st; rep from * to end. (40/48 sts)

**Round 6(7):** *1htr in each of next 7 sts, 2htr in next st; rep from * to end. (45/54 sts)

**Round 7(8):** *1htr in each of next 8 sts, 2htr in next st; rep from * to end. (50/60 sts)

**Round 8(9)-17(18):** 1htr in each st to end.

***Both sizes:***

Ss in next st. Fasten off.

## FINISHING
Make one large bobble with remaining yarn. Trim to approx 13cm (5in) diameter. Attach to top of hat.

DESIGN EIGHT

# BERRY CUSHION COVER

**Materials**
5 x 50g balls of Noro Kureyon, shade 329
52cm x 52cm (20½in x 20½ in) of Fabric Backing
51.5cm (20in) square cushion pad
Size 4.5mm crochet hook

**Size**
**Finished measurement:** 51.5cm (20in) square

**Tension**
13 sts and 7 rows to 10cm (4in) square working trebles using 4.5mm crochet hook.
It is essential to work to the correct tension. If there are less stitches, use a thinner hook, if there are more stitches, use a thicker hook.

**Abbreviations**

| | |
|---|---|
| **ch** | chain |
| **st(s)** | stitch(es) |
| **tr** | treble |
| **dc** | double |
| **yrh** | yarn round hook |
| **ch sp** | chain space |
| **rep** | repeat |
| **dtr/rf** | (double treble round front) dtr worked around stalk of st from previous round from front of work. Insert hook under the 'stalk' from right to left and complete dtr in usual way. |
| **tr5tog** | (treble five stitches together - bobble) yrh, insert hook into st, yrh, pull yarn through, yrh, pull yarn through 2 loops, *yrh, insert hook in same st, yrh, pull yarn through, yrh, pull yarn through 2 loops; rep from * 3 times more (6 loops on hook), yrh, pull yarn through all 6 loops, 1ch. (1tr5tog completed) |

## FRONT

**Base Row:** 60 ch, 1dc in each ch from hook (59 sts)

**Row 1:** 3ch (counts as first tr), 1tr in each of next 9 sts, *[1ch, miss 1 st, 1tr in next st] 3 times, ** 1tr in each of next 11 sts; rep from * ending last rep at **, 1tr in each of last 9 sts.

**Row 2:** 1ch, 1dc in each of next 10 sts, *tr5tog in next ch sp, 1dc in next tr, 1dc in next ch sp, 1dc in next tr, tr5tog in next sp, ** 1dc in each of next 12 sts; rep from *, ending last rep at **, 1dc in each of last 9 sts, 1dc in top of 3ch from previous Row.

**Row 3:** 3ch, miss 1 st, 1tr in each of next 5 sts, *1dtr/rf around next st (2 rows below, ie first row), 1tr in next st (of previous row), 1dtr/rf around next st (2 rows below), 1ch, miss 1 st, 1tr in next st (top of bobble), 1ch, miss 1 st, 1tr in next st, 1ch, 1tr in next st (top of bobble), 1ch, miss 1 st, 1dtr/rf around next st (2 rows below), 1tr in next st on previous row, 1dtr/rf around next st (2 rows below), ** 1tr in each of next 4 sts; rep from * ending last rep at **, 1tr in each of last 6 sts.

**Row 4:** 1ch, 1dc in each of next 9 sts, *1dc in next ch sp, 1dc in next st, 1dc in next ch sp, tr5tog in next st, 1dc in next ch sp, 1dc in next st, 1dc in next ch sp, ** 1dc in each of next 10 sts; rep from * ending last rep at **, 1dc in each of last 8 sts, 1dc in top of 3ch from previous Row.

**Row 5:** 3ch, miss first st, 1tr in each of first 5 sts, *1dtr/rf around next dtr, 1tr in next st, 1dtr/rf around next dtr, 1tr in next st, 1ch, miss 1 st, 1tr in next st, (stitch before bobble), 1ch, miss 1 st (bobble), 1tr in next st, (stitch after bobble), 1ch, miss 1 st, 1tr in next st, 1dtr/rf around next dtr, 1tr in next st, 1dtr/rf around next dtr, ** 1tr in each of next 4 sts; rep from * ending last rep at **, 1tr in each of last 6 sts.

Rep Rows 2-5 until work measures approx 51cm (19¾ in), ending on a Row 5.

**Next row:** 1ch, 1dc in each of next 10 sts, *[1dc in next ch sp, 1dc in next tr] 3 times, ** 1dc in each of next 11 sts; rep from * ending last rep at **, 1dc in each of last 8 sts, 1dc in top of 3ch from previous Row.

Fasten off.

## FINISHING

Measure, press and pin fabric allowing 1cm (½in) seam. With right sides together, pin and sew fabric backing to front crochet piece around three sides. Turn right side out. Insert cushion pad, sew up fourth side.

DESIGN NINE

# BOBBLE SCARF

**Materials**
5 x 50g balls of Noro Silk Garden, shade 389
Size 4.5mm crochet hook

**Size**
**Finished measurement:** 19cm x 126cm (7½in x 49½in)

**Tension**
13 sts and 7 rows to 10cm (4in) square working trebles using 4.5mm crochet hook.
It is essential to work to the correct tension. If there are less stitches, use a thinner hook, if there are more stitches, use a thicker hook.

**Abbreviations**

| | |
|---|---|
| **ch** | chain |
| **dc** | double crochet |
| **patt** | pattern |
| **rep** | repeat |
| **RS** | right side |
| **ss** | slip stitch |
| **st(s)** | stitch(es) |
| **tr** | treble |
| **yrh** | yarn round hook |
| **tr5CL** | (5 treble cluster) yrh, insert hook into st, yrh, pull yarn through, yrh, pull yarn through 2 loops, *yrh, insert hook in same st, yrh, pull yarn through, yrh, pull yarn through 2 loops; rep from * 3 times more (6 loops on hook), yrh, pull yarn through all 6 loops, 1ch. (1tr5CL completed) |

## SCARF

Make 32 ch.
**Base row: (WS)** 1dc in second chain from hook, 1dc in each ch to end.
**Next row:** 1ch, 1dc in each st to end.
Begin working in patt.
**Row 1: (WS)** 1ch, 1dc in first st, *[1tr5CL in next st, 1dc in each of next 3 sts]; rep from * to last 2 sts, 1tr5CL in next st, 1dc in last st.
**Row 2:** 1ch, 1dc in first st, *1dc in top of tr5CL, 1dc in each of next 3 sts; rep from * to last 2 sts, 1dc in top of next tr5CL, 1dc in last st.
**Row 3:** 1ch, *1dc in each of next 3 sts, tr5CL in next st; rep from * to last 3 sts, 1dc in each of last 3 sts.
**Row 4:** 1ch, *1dc in each of next 3 sts, 1dc in top of next tr5CL; rep from * to last 3 sts, 1dc in each of last 3 sts.
Rep last 4 rows until work measures 126cm (49½in) ending on a Row 2.
Fasten off.

## FINISHING

Sew in ends.

DESIGN TEN

# SHELL & LACE HEADBAND

**Materials**
1 x 50g ball of Noro Silk Garden 4ply, shade S373
Size 3mm crochet hook

**Size**
49cm x 12.5cm (19¼in x 4¾in)

**Tension**
18 sts and 9 rows to 10cm (4in) square working trebles using 3mm crochet hook.
It is essential to work to the correct tension. If there are less stitches, use a thinner hook, if there are more stitches, use a thicker hook.

**Abbreviations**

| | |
|---|---|
| **ch** | chain |
| **ch sp** | chain space |
| **dc** | double crochet |
| **htr** | half treble |
| **rep** | repeat |
| **RS** | right side |
| **st(s)** | stitch(es) |
| **sp** | space |
| **tr** | treble |
| **WS** | wrong side |

## HEADBAND

Make 32 ch.
**Row 1: (RS)** 1dc in second ch from hook, 1dc in next ch, *miss 3ch, work a Fan of [3tr, 1ch, 3tr] in next ch, miss 3ch, 1dc in next ch **, 1ch, miss 1ch, 1dc in next ch; rep from * ending last rep at **, 1dc in last ch.
**Row 2:** 2ch (counts as 1htr), 1htr in first st *2ch, 1dc in ch sp at centre of next Fan, 2ch**, work a V st of [1htr, 1ch, 1htr] in ch sp between 2dcs from previous row; rep from * ending last rep at **, 2htr into last dc.
**Row 3:** 3ch, 3tr in first st, *1dc in next 2ch sp, 1ch, 1dc in next 2ch sp **, work a Fan into ch sp at centre of next V st; rep from * ending last rep at **, 4tr in top of 2ch from previous row.
**Row 4:** 1ch, 1dc in first st, *2ch, V st in next ch sp between 2dcs from previous row, 2ch**, 1dc in ch sp at centre of next Fan; rep from * ending last rep at **, 1dc in top of 3ch from previous row.
**Row 5:** 1ch, 1dc in first st, *1dc in next ch sp, work a Fan into ch sp at centre of next V st, 1dc in next ch sp **, 1ch; rep from * ending last rep at **, 1dc in 1ch from previous row.
Rep Rows 2 to 5 until work measures 49cm (19¼in) ending on a Row 2.
Fasten off.

## HEADBAND GATHERING STRAP

Make 14 ch.
**Row 1:** 1htr in third ch from hook (first 2 ch counts as htr), 1htr in each ch to end. (13 sts)
**Row 2:** 2ch (counts as htr), 1htr in each htr to end. (14 sts)
Rep Row 2 seven times more, or until strap measures approx 7½cm (3in).
Fasten off.

## FINISHING

With right sides facing, sew ends of headband together.
Turn right side out.
Fold headband gathering strap around the headband so it covers the seam and join the ends of the strap together.
Twist strap around so its seam is inside the headband.

DESIGN ELEVEN

# DEVINE DEVICE COVER

**Materials**

1 x 50g ball of Noro Kureyon shade 287
2 large press studs /snap fasteners
1 leather tassel
Lining fabric (to fit finished crocheted piece, plus seam allowances)
Size 4mm crochet hook

**Size**

Measurements of our device (iPad):
24cm (9½in) width, 18.5cm (7¼in) length

**Tension**

13 sts and 7 rows to 10cm (4in) square working trebles using 4mm crochet hook.
It is essential to work to the correct tension. If there are less stitches, use a thinner hook, if there are more stitches, use a thicker hook.

**Pattern Note**

Measure the length and the width of the device. This pattern is based on an iPad measuring approximately 24cm x 18.5cm x .9cm (9½in x 7¼in x ½in), but use the tension as a guide to make a base chain to measure the width of your device and continue until the length matches the length of your device. If your device is much bigger you will need more yarn.
If you need to alter the amount of stitches, calculate a multiple of 6 sts, plus 1 for the shell pattern, plus another 1 for the base chain.

**Abbreviations**

| | |
|---|---|
| **ch** | chain |
| **ch sp** | chain space |
| **dc** | double crochet |
| **htr** | half treble |
| **rep** | repeat |
| **RS** | right side |
| **ss** | slip stitch |
| **st(s)** | stitch(es) |
| **sp** | space |
| **tr** | treble |
| **WS** | wrong side |

## FRONT AND BACK (both alike)

Using 4mm hook, make 38 ch.

**Base row:** 1dc in second ch from hook, 1dc in each ch to end. (37 sts)

**Next row:** 1ch, 1dc in each st to end.

## SHELL PATTERN

**Row 1:** 1ch, 1dc in first st, *miss 2 sts, 5tr in next st, miss 2 sts, 1dc in next st; rep from * to end. (6 shell groups)

**Row 2:** 3ch, 2tr in first st, *miss next 2 sts, 1dc in next st (centre of shell group), miss next 2 sts, 5tr in next dc (between shells); rep from * ending 3tr in last dc.

**Row 3:** 1ch, 1dc in first st, *miss 2 sts, 5tr in next dc, miss 2 sts, 1dc in next st; rep from * ending 1dc in top of 3ch. (6 shell groups)

Rep Rows 2 and 3 until work measures approx 19cm (7½in) finishing on a Row 2.

**Next row:** 1ch, 1dc in each of first 2 sts, *1htr in next tr, 1tr in next dc, 1htr in next tr, 1dc in each of next 3 tr; rep from * to last 2 tr, 1htr in next tr, 1dc in last tr, 1dc in top of 3ch.

Fasten off.

Repeat for other side.

## FINISHING

Block and steam Front and Back to make them the same size.

Place the Front and Back crochet pieces RS together and join side and bottom seams. Turn RS out.

Measure the finished crochet pieces and allowing measurements for the length, width and depth of the device add 3cm (1¼in) to these dimensions and cut the lining fabric into two pieces.

Place the lining pieces RS together and pin along sides and bottom edges. Sew the sides and bottom with a 1.5cm (¾in) seam. Press seams open.

Fold 1.5cm (¾in) (or to fit) to WS along top edge and press.

Place the lining inside the crochet piece WS together.

Pin and hand sew the top edge of the lining to the top edge of the crochet piece using a sewing needle and neutral thread.

Sew press studs /snap fasteners onto each side of lining, in centre near top.

Add leather tassel (if required).

DESIGN TWELVE

# HYDRANGEA TABLECLOTH

**Materials**

8 x 50g balls of Noro Taiyo 4ply, shade 3

Size 4.5mm and 5mm crochet hooks

**Size**

**Approximately** 102cm (40in) square

**Abbreviations**

| | |
|---|---|
| **approx** | approximately |
| **ch** | chain |
| **ch sp** | chain space |
| **dc** | double crochet |
| **cont** | continu(e)(ing) |
| **RS** | right side |
| **ss** | slip stitch |
| **st(s)** | stitch(es) |
| **tr** | treble |
| **2trCL Picot** | (Two Treble Cluster Picot) [yrh, insert hook in st (or sp), yrh, pull yarn through, yrh, pull yarn through first 2 loops on hook] twice in same st (or sp), yrh, pull yarn through all 3 loops on hook. |

**Tension**

18 sts and 9 rows to 10cm (4in) square working trebles using 4.5mm crochet hook.

It is essential to work to the correct tension. If there are less stitches, use a thinner hook, if there are more stitches, use a thicker hook.

## TABLECLOTH

Using size 5mm, make 146 ch.

**Row 1:** Change to a size 4.5mm hook, 1dc in 2nd ch from hook, *miss 2 ch, 5tr in next ch (shell made), miss 2 ch, 1tr in next ch; rep from * ending with 1dc (instead of 1tr) in last ch.

**Row 2: (WS)** 3ch, 2tr in first st (half shell), *miss 2 tr, 1tr in centre tr of shell, miss next 2 tr (remainder of shell)**, 5tr in next tr (between shells); rep from * ending last rep at **, 3tr in last st.

**Row 3: (RS)** 1ch, 1tr in first tr, miss 2 tr, *5tr in next tr**, miss 2tr, 1tr in centre tr shell; rep from * ending last rep at **, 1tr in top of 3ch.

Repeat Rows 2 and 3 until a total of 76 rows have been worked, ending on a Row 2.

Do not fasten off.

## EDGING

To achieve evenly placed stitches along sides, add pin markers. Start by putting a pin marker at the centre point along the side, then another pin marker between the end and the central pin marker and so on, thus dividing the side into quarters. Then divide the total amount of sts needed for each side into 4. (eg: 140 dc = 35 dc in each quarter). This makes it easier to get an even result.

**Round 1:** Working on WS and starting along the side edge, 1ch, 3dc in top of last tr from last Row. (Corner made). Make 140 dc evenly to next corner. (See Tip). * 3dc in next corner st, 140 dc evenly along next edge to next corner; rep from * twice more, end with a ss in first dc. Fasten off. Turn.

**Round 2:** Working on RS. Join yarn in second st to left of last corner st. 3ch (counts as 1tr), *1tr in each of next 2 sts, [5ch, miss 5 sts, 1tr in next st, 5ch, miss 5 sts, 1tr in each of next 3 sts] to one st before corner st. 3ch, miss 1 st, 1tr in corner st, 3ch, miss 1tr, ** 1tr in next st; rep from * ending last rep at **, join with a ss in top of first 3ch.

**Round 3:** 3ch (counts as 1tr), *1tr in each of next 2tr, 3ch, [(1tr, 3ch, 1tr) in next tr, 3ch, 1tr in each of next 3 tr, 3ch] to next corner st, [1tr, 3ch, 1tr] in next tr (corner group made), 3ch, ** 1tr in next tr; rep from * ending last rep at **, join with a ss in top of first 3ch.

**Round 4:** 3ch (counts as 1tr), *1tr in next 2tr, 2ch, [miss 1tr, 7tr in next ch sp, 2ch, miss 1 tr, 1tr in each of next 3 tr, 2ch] to next corner group, 9tr in corner 3ch sp (corner group made), 2ch, miss 1 tr, ** 1tr in next tr; rep from * ending last rep at **, join with a ss in top of first 3ch.

**Round 5:** 3ch (counts as 1tr), *1tr in each of next 2tr, 1ch, [(2trCL Picot in next tr, 2ch, miss 1tr) three times, 2trCL Picot in next tr, 1ch, 1tr in each of next 3 tr, 1ch] to next corner group, [2trCL Picot, 2ch, miss 1 tr] 4 times, 2trCL Picot in next tr, 1ch, ** 1tr in next tr; rep from * ending last rep at **, join with a ss in top of first 3ch.

## FINISHING

Sew in ends.

DESIGN THIRTEEN

# SUMMER GARDEN THROW

## Materials

10 x 50g balls of Noro Silk Garden Lite shade 2073
Size 4mm crochet hook

## Size

**Finished measurement:**
92.5cm x 87.5cm (36½in x 34½in)

## Tension

14 sts and 11 rows to 10cm (4in) square working trebles using 4mm crochet hook.
It is essential to work to the correct tension. If there are less stitches, use a thinner hook, if there are more stitches, use a thicker hook.

## Abbreviations

| | |
|---|---|
| **ch** | chain |
| **ch sp** | chain space |
| **st** | stitch |
| **yrh** | yarn round hook |
| **dc** | double crochet |
| **htr** | half treble |
| **ss** | slip stitch |
| **tr** | treble |
| **Puff** | *yrh, insert hook in st, yrh, pull yarn through st, and draw up a 2.5cm (1in) loop; rep from * 3 more times, yrh and draw through 9 loops on hook. |

## SQUARES (make 21)

Work 4 ch, join with a ss to form a ring.

**Round 1:** 1ch, 8dc into ring, ss into first dc.

**Round 2:** Draw yarn up to make a 2.5cm (1in) loop. Make a puff in same st, 3ch, [1 Puff, 3ch] in next st 7 times more, ss in top of first Puff. (8 Puffs)

**Round 3:** Ss in next ch sp. 3ch, (counts as 1tr), 3tr into same ch sp, *5tr in next ch sp, 4tr in next ch sp; rep from * to last ch sp, 5tr in last ch sp, ss in top of first 3ch.

**Round 4:** 3ch (counts as 1tr), 1tr in each of next 5 sts, *3tr in next st, (corner) 1tr in each of next 8 sts; rep from * to last 3 sts, 3tr in next st, 1tr in each of last 2 sts, ss in top of first 3ch.

**Round 5:** 3ch (counts as 1tr), 1tr in each of next 6 sts, * [3tr, 1ch, 3tr] in next st (centre of 3tr group from previous Round), 1tr into each of next 10 sts; rep from * to last 4 sts, [3tr, 1ch, 3tr] in next st, 1tr in each of last 3 sts, ss in top of first 3ch.

Fasten off.

Sew in ends.

## FLOWERS (make 21)

Work 4 ch, join with a ss to form a ring.

**Round 1:** 1ch, 8dc into ring, ss into first dc.

**Round 2:** 1ch, 1dc in same dc, 2ch [1dc in next st, 2ch] 7 times, join with a ss in first dc. (8 ch sps)

**Round 3:** Ss in first 2ch sp, 1ch, [1dc, 1htr, 1dc] in same sp, [1dc, 1htr, 1dc] in next 2ch sp 7 times, join with a ss in back of first dc. (8 petals)

**Round 4:** Working behind petals [3ch, ss] behind first dc of next petal 7 times, 3ch, join with a ss in first 3ch. (8 ch sps)

**Round 5:** Working in ch sps behind petals, [1dc, 3htr, 1dc] in next 3 ch sp 8 times, join with a ss in back of first dc. (8 petals)

**Round 6:** Working behind petals, [5ch, ss behind first dc of next petal] 7 times, 5ch, join with a ss in first 3ch. (8 ch sps)

**Round 7:** Working in ch sps behind petals, [1dc, 2htr, 3tr, 2htr, 1dc] in next 5ch sp 8 times, join with a ss in back of first dc. (8 petals)

**Round 8:** Working behind petals, [6ch, ss behind first dc of next petal] 7 times, 6ch, join with a ss in first of 3ch. (8 ch sps)

**Round 9:** Working in ch sps behind petals, [1dc, 2htr, 5tr, 2htr, 1dc] in next 6ch sp, 8 times, join with a ss in back of first dc. (8 petals).

Fasten off.

## FINISHING

Sew in ends. Alternating squares and flowers, lay them out: 7 pieces (length) x 6 pieces (width).

With wrong sides together, join the tips of 2 petals on each edge to the edges of the squares.

# HOOKED ON NORO

## DISTRIBUTORS *For details of Noro Yarns stockists please contact:*

**FRANCE**
Plassard Diffusion,
La Filature, 71800 Varennes-sous-Dun,
Tel: +33 (0)3 85282828 Fax: +33 (0) 385282829
E-mail: info@laines-plassard.com

**AUSTRALIA / NEW ZEALAND**
Prestige Yarns Pty Ltd
Unit 6, 8-10 Pioneer Drive, Bellambi NSW 2518 Tel: +61 24 285 6669
Email: info@prestige yarns.com www.prestigeyarns.com

**JAPAN**
Eisaku Noro & Co Ltd
55 Shimoda Ohibino Azaichou, Ichinomiya Aichi, 491 0105
Tel: +81 586 51 3113 Fax: + 81 586 51 2625
Email: noro@io.ocn.ne.jp www.eisakunoro.com

**RUSSIA – FOR LENINGRAD AREA**
Fashion Needlework,
Evgenia Rodina, Ul. Nalichnaya, 27, St Petersburg 199226.
Tel no: +7 (812) 928-17-39, (812) 350-56-76, (911) 988-60-03.
E-mail: knitting.info@gmail.com. Www.fashion-rukodelie.ru

**RUSSIA – EXCLUDING LENINGRAD AREA**
Praimar Hobby, LLC
129343, Serebryakova Proezd, 14B, Moscow
Tel no: +7 (495) 225-0810
E-mail: sales.praimar@gmail.com Web: noro.praimar.ru

**ITALY**
Lucia Fornasari
Via Cuniberti, 22 Ivrea (TO) 10015
Contact: Lucia Fornasari Tel no: + 39 345 566 5568
E-mail: info@lavoroamaglia.it www.lavoroamaglia.it

**GERMANY / AUSTRIA / SWITZERLAND / BENELUX**
Designer Yarns (Deutschland) GMBH
Welserstrasse 10g, D-51149 Koln
Tel: +49 (0) 2203 1021910 Fax: +49 (0) 2203 1023551
E-mail: info@designeryarns.de

**SWEDEN**
Hamilton Yarns
Storgatan 14, 64730 Mariefred
Tel/Fax: +46 (0) 1591 2006 www.hamiltondesign.biz

**FINLAND**
Eiran Tukku,
Makelankatu 54B, 00510 Helsinki. Tel no: +358 503460575.
E-mail: maria.hellbom@eirantukku.fi

**NORWAY**
Viking of Norway,
Bygdaveien 63, 4333 Oltedal.
Tel: +47 51611660 Fax: +47 51616235,
E-mail: post@viking-garn.no. www.viking-garn.no